I Wonder if You Will Ponder?

A collection of poems

By

Rudy Calderón M.A.

ISBN: 1-4107-9211-0 (e-book)
ISBN: 1-4107-9210-2 (Paperback)

Library of Congress Control Number: 2003096007

This book is printed on acid free paper.

Printed in the United States of America
Bloomington, IN

1stBooks - rev. 11/10/03

Special Dedication

I would like to dedicate this book to some important people in my life. First, a big part of this book is dedicated to my oldest nephew Raul Garcia Jr. I have the deepest respect for him as a strong Christian soldier who found his spiritual and existential armor in 2002/2003. I stand by you always in your present situation. All love from your uncle, who is there for you through it all and in all tribulations. You are going to be someone that makes a great contribution to our society and someone I will look up to and will ask for guidance. Stay strong and always keep your focus and never lose your beliefs and values.

I would also like to, in a very special way, thank my dear mother, Ana M. Vasquez. She has been the pillar that I have leaned on throughout my life. I'm thankful to her because she was able to provide us the essentials and an unconditional love that, I'm sure, is acknowledged by all my brothers and sisters. My step dad, Abel Vasquez, has also played a pivotal role in giving me sound advice and motivation to pursue my goals. I wish to also thank and acknowledge my dear brothers and sisters: Felipe, Maria, Jose, Leticia, George, Rosalinda, and Richard. I would also like to thank my cousin Martha Calderón and family for their support. To my nephew, Hector Munguia, as well as my other nephews and nieces I wish to awaken their hidden potentials and talents that I know they have. I would also like to thank a dear friend (S.N.) for being an important friend at an important stage in my life; she helped inspire some of these love poems. I wish you all the luck in your endeavor and know you will succeed.

I want you guys and whom ever I have left out, to know that you are truly appreciated and very important in giving the moral support to allow this book to come to fruition. Please know that I am forever grateful for having you in my life.

About the Author

Rudy Calderón was born in the metropolis of Los Angeles, CA in December of 1974. He is the sixth of eight children and a first generation Mexican-American. His family moved to Santa Maria, CA as migrant workers to pick strawberries, lettuce, and squash, where they finally settled and have since remained. Rudy attended most of the elementary schools in Santa Maria and later attended El Camino Jr. High School. He went on to graduate from Santa Maria High School and then attended Allan Hancock College. He, then, transferred to Cal State University, Bakersfield, where he was deeply empowered by the history, philosophy and political science departments. He graduated in 2001 (*Cum Laude*) with a major in history and minor in political science. After graduation, he returned to Santa Maria, where he enrolled and received his California teaching credential and masters degree in the field of education from Chapman University. Email: rcal67@hotmail.com

Table of Contents

Society/Life

Love

Society/Life

I Wonder if You Will Ponder?
A collection of poems

I wonder if you will ponder?

I wonder how many days must there go by without any peace?
Or people at ease,
Especially in the Middle East?
When will the fighting cease?
Man, so many unnecessarily deceased

We all try to be good to one another
But often times only bring grief to our mothers

I wonder why all the murders?
Whether it was 2pac or Biggie, JFK, MLK, or Gandhi
Haven't we learned how not to be?
These people lost their lives trying to get us to see
Of a better dream
That was meant for you and me

All the hommies from around the block try to do good deep down
But with all the peer pressure around
If they tried to do good, they would never live it down
Or be left to be called clowns

I wonder where is the justice?
A kid from around the block who minded his own
But to show you of the evil of people be known
Was attacked by three men grown,
Who showed him no mercy as they broke his bones
Just to be known
What a crazy people who will ultimately reap what they've sewn

I wonder if compassion has ears to hear?
I would tell it that this society screams for a better reality
That if we don't change, will only lead to live a life of brutality
It is my wish that we see and agree to believe,
THEN more importantly fight to achieve
Only then will there be relief
I wonder if you will ponder?

3

My Gratitude to the Art of Writing

My gratitude goes out to the art of writing
Whether its prose or poems
That gives way to our minds to roam
Because in the past whenever our hearts have needed guidance
We have gone to those we confide in
Whether it's Cornel West, Frost, Emerson, Tony Morrison, or
Thoreau
They have taught us of the things to we should fix our sight on
and in what to say no
Because some things can be meaningless
And won't give our soul console

It's through this art of writing that I
Can express my truest feelings
And in that my soul is relieving
Because these verses extend an open ear
To this pen that consumes and releases many lonely tears

Through these poems that I write,
My heart and soul get a better sight
A sight that helps me make sense of so much plight,
And from there I can begin doing what is right

When my pen begins to spill ink,
That's when my pride it does sink
And my mind begins to throw out words and advice
That in the past I have read and heard
And at first they sound absurd
But after some thinking
The message it does start sinking

In my reflective writing,
That is when my pen does rejoice and is not hiding
And my thoughts begin to fly like a kite

And I begin to understand what it is that I must do right
Hopefully, a wise message can come as I write
So I may walk in a much brighter light
And be able to use hindsight
So that in my future actions,
I can sleep better at night

June 13, 2003

Was 2pac the poet of compassion?

Was 2pac the poet of compassion?
Yeah he was the type to be lashin'
Especially when he saw injustice, oh yeah he'd start mashin'
On behalf of the people that he saw down in the hole
He felt their pain burn like a coal
Because the elite did not care to console
Console them in their times of difficulty because of course the
system in place you know the "status quo"
Was a system where people should learn to know their role
But behold this black man said "hell no!"
And wasn't afraid to speak the truth so that our
Humanity and compassion could grow
Even though the message to those at the top sounded violent
It spoke of the poverty and the fact that a disproportionate amount
of minorities were struggling just to pay rent
So it was, you see, a way for them, through him, vent
"T.H.U.G. L.I.F.E." was the acronym he chose to fight for and
that he diagnosed
The social issues of the time he looked at real close
Because he felt that at the end of the nonsense there was a red rose
He had an affinity to blacks
And their suffering that's why he wrote voraciously,
Which you can see by all the poems and songs of
Compassion that if put together would
Create big stacks
And to many this message
Was received kindly
So their loyalty and love
He will never, even
In his grave, lack

March 14, 2003

The Struggle

The struggle for peace is a never-ending battle that takes many
lives
And creates many widows out of former wives
Such a shame that we can't create harmonious states
The consequences of it leaves us at times without our precious
mates
If we haven't learned from the death toll
Gone before
Then it leaves me wondering does the U.S.
Really know what it's fighting for?
Oh, that's right natural resources
That is a big motivator so say my sources
Arab hegemony over the oil
Causes the U.S. blood to boil
So they work and toil
To get that precious resource, while recruiting
Those who don't question the government but show they are loyal
That's the quality that the government looks at as royal
That is not to say that Saddam gives a damn.
He might carry resentment and want to get even with Uncle Sam
It is no secret that he is a prudent and autocratic person
But if we were to attack all the autocrats then, in our country, why
aren't we cursin'?
If your tears feel like burstin'
Because of your patriotic fervor then you have it all wrong cause
you
See I'm not a boastin'
I love my country but not at the expense of looking over things
That can cut off her precious wings
Critical analysis is a must
Make sure you don't just look at sensitive issues only at the crust
Look for peace because it will allow us to live more happily
Hopefully until we are deceased

It is my hope that we can work to release the grips of hatred and
animosity
Which if not let go will bring about brutality
Let us work together in this world community
Keep your eyes on the ultimate prize
Whether believer of the word
Or those that have never heard
And think that this type of belief is absurd

March 3, 2003

It's the 4th of July

It's the 4th of July but why do I cry?
Just listening to those fireworks, I can't help but to sigh
You see there's a dear nephew of mine
That because of wrongfully taking these things
He's behind bars for many years caught in a bind
Treated by the criminal system in a way that is not kind
And oh I know, I know! If he could he would
Turn back the hands of time
Oh that clock, how I too wish I could rewind
Because he does not deserve the punishment
That to him was given
Can't they see that his precious time, out in this world,
He was barely beginning?

It's the 4th of July so why must I lie?
Why must I lie and say to many people that justice is as sweet as a
pie?
When deep down inside
Those judges' faces on my "good list" they could never reside
Because right now I cannot calmly sit back
And this dear nephew of mine how his presence I do lack

It's the 4th of July of 2003
But I'm consoled because the next day
The noise is no more
And the pain of this holiday, I do not feel to my core
I hope you feel me and understand these lamentable bitter verses
Sometimes I feel that the California Judicial system they do hear
my curses
If that is achieved, then I'll be relieved
With time, this nephew of mine
Will come home and his own

9

Family and dreams
Fully achieve

July 4th, 2003

History

History offers us much to look back on
If we navigate under the surface
We'll find that some topics are as hot as a furnace
But still we must learn from the lessons that teach us
They teach us to be as nice as we can
Not just to our fellow man
But to everything in this land
And that in what we strongly believe in
We should take a stand
Do you understand?
The Chinese and Cubans and Mexican people
all fight for one thing and
That's to be equal

March 3, 2003

What Will You Do To Be Free?

What will you do to be free?
Will you stand up to the powers that be?
Or will you stand by like a spectator and just see
See that in the streets there's little relief
And the question that I ask you, is will you look for the key
To unleash the masses of people in dire situations
Allowing them to feel more positive sensations?

Will you fight or will there be flight?
Your answer to this question will either show your might
Or the fact that you have no vision or sight
To stand up to what is right.
If you follow the status quo,
Will you end up negatively reaping what you sew?

Always fight to be free from being marginalized in this society
To show that in our community there are many
Willing to fight for the piety
So always fight for what is right
Even if you have to work and toil all through the night
To Cesar Chavez and Jessie De La Cruz, that would be a beautiful
sight
So this positive uplifting message my brother or sister always try
and send
Because in the end
That's the only way that your
Heart can truly mend

June 13, 2003

How will you use your education?

Hey my man, they say you're educated
But how much does that prove to your fellow woman or man?
Does it prove that you have what it takes
To bring out emotions in people that will make them feel elated?
Have you been listening to what has just been stated?
Yeah, you with your B.A., M.A. or PhD
Are you listening to my decree?
Or will you never see?
I know people really deep down want to use the
Knowledge to plant good seeds
But many times that does more to remind us of
Our imperfections as human beings
So much that I've read about our world
I'm telling you sometimes it all seems absurd
Because some of our leaders and diplomats
Have in the past and to this day
Laid down our lives at the front steps of war
To even some economic score
That will create many lonely moms holding their
Sons or daughters picture and
Unleashing a motherly roar
If their education is used only to kill
Many will think that their university professors
Were nothing more than some
Old run of the mill
Then as I see those appetitive business merchants
With their MBAs, yeah they do much hurtin'
Do they feel the hunger as they're taking
Unrightfully from all those poor families?
Or do those ethical questions not matter
In their financial quest?
Then I will say that your education and
Morality was sometime ago
Laid to rest

May this message fall on opened ears

Christianity what does that mean?
It's about loving the Christ all through the week
So please try and seek
Seek the one that redeems,
When you feel him you'll be on the best team
And it'll at times feel just like a dream

To all my atheist friends
Who try and pretend
That what I'm saying makes nonsense
Then I will plead for you to believe
Because that's the missing ingredient you see

To all my agnostic friends
You neither believe
Nor say that we're being deceived
So I tell you that the one that relieves
Is waiting for you to
Calm all your needs

To the whole world at large
Please lend an ear
To the God that is dear
He's dear and he wants us to be near
If you put your trust in our savior
Believe me he'll change for the better your behavior

March 4, 2003

Great Christian Soldiers

If small in stature David defeated the giant Goliath with the help
of God,
How can people sit there and in disbelief nod?
Nod as if he doesn't exist
Haven't they've seen the giants that he uplifts?

Whether it was Moses or Abraham or the Philippian people,
God has helped those that have gone to the steeple

Abraham, the great patriarch
Did everything God asked, he'd have even built what Noah did,
you know the ark
Abraham was a towering soldier
That's why he's a beacon
That the people came seekin'

St. Paul was a man that, at first, was confused
Until he fell off the mule
Which God used as a tool
When St. Paul saw the light and was saved,
He fought for the Lord
And Christianity's road he did pave
From the book of Romans to Ephesians to the book of Philemon
What he wanted was to tell us about home
Not the home from this world because this is absurd
But the home
That makes one never experience the feeling as if they're alone

April 27, 2003

Adapt

The art of being adaptive
Is essential in a world that can make one feel like a captive
But adapt in a way that one doesn't lose their beliefs
And leads to a life of addiction
Whether it is alcohol, violence or stealing
Which all in their extreme can lead to much killings

Adapt is a term Darwin learned well
Even though that theory of his it does itself smell
He understood that humans must be resilient
Resilient to circumstances that could pit us in any situation
There a person would be forced to act for their own protection

So people all over this world please learn from history and other
people's lives
That in the end what one does and says is motivated by the goal to
survive
Even if one has to live near a bee hive
Handle your business and your time do not let it go to waste
But adapt and act in a way that you can finish the race
The race in this life and move on and in the end leave all this strife
To be in a better place where this word will have no meaning
In this belief I will go out screaming

March 18, 2003

Judge—Are You a Man?

Judge—are you a man?
Why did you not do your job? I know that you can
If the person under question was named Dan
And if he were the quote unquote "crook,"
Would that change your outlook?
I hope to God that that's not the case
Because then I would think that this criminal
Court case system is such a waste

Twelve years for a crime that had no one hurt
And no one can pinpoint my nephew, does that make
You a little bit curious about the case?
If not, that makes me furious to think that
Your intellect, in this case,
Seems like such a waste

What did you say?
What was his record you ask?
Clean, nothing before this and still you want to overlook this?
It's obvious that that the legislators and judges in California,
With regards to sensitive cases like these, have no ears to hear
I'm convinced that the very angels say in their minds, "Oh dear!"
But Tulare County's court system is quite clear
This cities court system is sending its future generations
To sit for many years in a cell,
That will make these reparable youth later look at the legislators
and yell
And later the apathy they will feel
Believe you me it will be for real
If this system and these laws are not adjudicated and alleviated,
It will create within our beautiful nation an unfortunate schism
And a society even more truncated
Have you listened to what has been stated?

16

Let's not make these laws such
That they'll send this world toward a legalism
So extreme it will only create a world of no value
Otherwise known as nihilism

March 9, 2003

Madness in the System

There is a madness in the California court system
It has flaws and makes the American people especially those that
are socially conscious feel that people are set up
Set up to do a sentence that is enough to make people feel fed up

Why does a seventeen-year old, nephew of mine *Raul Garcia Jr.*
Have to be dealt with so cold?
From a system that is so unfair that
It's justice smells like mold
If you understand me good, if not then behold
Because I'm at a point in my analysis where I will begin to scold
Scold all those who sat there and litigated
These devilish and inhumane laws,
Who do they think they are God?

Yeah, you lean back in your chair Mr. Legislator
But hey sometimes what you do or write comes back to bite you
later
And your actions you'll deal, on an individual basis, with your
creator

God will ultimately bring justice to this strong nephew of mine
Because he is a good man
Raised in the hood
But through it all stood
And will show how he could overcome the hatred of this system
that if it doesn't realize its flaws
Will never realize that it is trapped
in the evil Man's jaws

March 9, 2003

Why so many Mexicans in jail?

Why so many Mexicans in jail?
This I ask to you my Lord
Many are just clinging on their last string
You know, their last cord
And the thought of so many suicides lets me know that
The pain that these youth face society can no longer hide
That's why I resort to poetry to expose this negative side
Because this is the place where the truth can be allowed to speak
In the hopes that we can as a society be more compassionate and
So we can wrestle with the notion of being meek
And for a better future hopefully seek
So many brown skins behind bars
Sitting there wishing to go back to their block
And the thoughts that roam through their minds is being
Able to once again cruise in their cars
And to finally walk in the right path and
Shoot for the stars
That's what they tell their mothers
Who never paid attention to them as kids
But now behind bars they want to their
son/daughter with love smother
Lord, will Hispanics be treated fairly in these "Correctional
facilities"
Or will they be left to survive in a rat race
Where injustice and backstabbing will be the case
And if they do good,
Will committee's decision leave in these youths a bad taste?
If that's the case
Then what is the meaning of value to them?
Resentment and coldness will make them nihilistic
And from then on that reparable youth will
For society carry a deep resentment
Oh legislator, you say that they'll be treated more fairly in Y.A.
Let's ask my brothers there and see what they say

Some of those youth can do the most harm
Because the block has now created more pressures and less
education
Thus creating less consciousness
So to stab and eliminate you
Is something that these unemotional machines
Have been registered to do
So that they negatively pursue

Happy Home

A happy home is what I need
That is what allows people to succeed
And in their goals more easily proceed

A happy home won't allow my mind to roam
Roam to the mentally crippling corners of my mind

A happy home lets me live a life that excludes
Much pain and madness,
Which in the end only equates
to sadness
I need to start feeling some of
Those better emotions
Like that much needed caress
Once someone has that,
Then in everything else they do
They can begin to do their best
Which is the ultimate
Quest

Is it better at the top?

Is it better at the top?
What an interesting question
Is it the color of my skin
That I use to measure my sin?
No, that I'm convinced cannot be the answer
So then how do we make sense of so much disaster?
Make sense of the disaster that we see
And the disproportional levels of wealth?
To level the field can we somehow this economic latter melt?
And if I do one day make it to the top,
Will I have to change my attitude and
My virtuous ways somehow stop?
Not to say that I am perfect by any stretch of the imagination
I just need to know if I do make it
Will I become enslaved to the temptations?
That to me is my great fear
Because I do not want to lose that part of me that is sincere
So still I ask is it better up there?
I know I hear that the people up there do care
Even as they look down and to the people down there
Very few times want to look at
And into their eyes stare
It is hard to fathom in this capitalist country that
This virtuosity is running around
Because it is truly rare

Estudia

La escuela es algo necesario para progresar
Y hoy, para no oír me, no vallas a tosar
Porque te voy a rogar
Que para un mejor y alegre hogar
Te quiero sugerir que pongas todas
tus ganas a estudiar

Entiende que con la educación viene mas lana
Y te puedo apostar que eso te aconseja tu mamá
Con la educación se ganará mas facil el dinero
que andar piscando caña
Por la mañana

Qualquiera que sea la materia
Puedes triunfar y si al principio no puedes
no te me pongas serio o seria
Mejor ven a la biblioteca y al irte te vas a ir con mas alegria
Si no me crees entonces preguntale
a tu amiga

11 de Marzo 2003

Men do Cry

Men do cry
That's a matter of fact
It happens because they're not afraid to be real
So they come forth and reveal
They reveal their compassion but many women
See them and cannot ration
That we are humans beings of flesh and blood
They don't think that crying should come from a man
But if even the Man from above cried,
Then women would understand that it's okay
And would understand it
Being able to show one's humanity
Is a quality that helps keep
Many men's sanity

March 11, 2003

Noon Tutoring

Ladies and Gentlemen come on in and sit down
I know you're feeling down
Because you're in here
But oh it's not so bad so that you have to shed a tear
But please don't frown
We won't let you down
Just think of the prize at the end of the year
you know it has to do with a gown

Just know that this time in hear will lead you towards the right
route
Oh, and one of my rules please don't shout
Or else you'll be thrown out
And believe me you don't want to go that route
So get your homework and class work out
And let us know how we can help you out

March 16, 2003

Mexico's Labyrinth

Is the Mexican's mind in a labyrinth?
So claimed one Nobel Peace Prize winner Octavio Paz
I can understand where he's coming from because
I've observed what he said many Mexicans have in their mind
Which many might interpret as inaccurate and unkind
He called it the great distrust
Which, in the Mexican, cannot only be seen at the crust
But deep analysis into their history is a must
A labyrinth of tremendous proportions
That if by the Mexican not deciphered can lead
To a life of unfortunate distortions
But today whether right or wrong
Mexico moves along if need be singing a song
And searching for a life of hedonism
That is the most long

March 11, 2003

Pain

How does one deal with the pain?
Of not being able to gain
The pleasure and positive right of having the essentials or security
To allow you to relax, while observing the rain and
Nature in all its purity

I know that there are many like me
That grew up feeling the heat
In the home and out in the street
The pressure was building day in and day out
Making this brother just want to break out
Break out of this never-ending world wind
Making him wonder were they so bad my sins?

Raised with nothing but broken dreams was tough
Which led to disheartenment and forced this young kid's heart
to become hardened
And when your dad leaves the home you know
It gives way for your thoughts to roam
And many times those thoughts come back to
Remind you that you're all alone
Oh! how the scorn makes you feel torn
And it's then that a flood of thoughts hit me just like a storm
And I'm left wondering "Could I have had a better home?"

Please help me Lord and remove this pain, which is like a veil
So then I can see and move on and be the person you called to
prevail
And not fall victim to the criminal system, which it is in itself in
so many ways criminal
I don't want to land in jail
Without a chance at bail

And left to contact my loved ones only by mail
But more importantly have my dreams jump on
A ship and forever set sail

March 11, 2003

Problems

I know we all have problems
Who knows where they start?
Or where begins their stems?
Are these problems all caused by men?
That's an interesting question
Being a man, do I regret that this I did mention?
No, not really, but if you're a guy
I know that now your ears they do listen

Are your problems the same or worse than mine?
You know that question can never be answered
Because we all have and are put in different situations
That makes the answer to this question
Insurmountable even under deep contemplation
In all our problems just smile
All the while
Keeping your sense of style
That way in your mind the problems
Won't seem like a big pile
And if that doesn't work my ear and heart is
Open so please my number dial

April 3, 2003

Sunshine

Sunshine in the air
Is quite debonair
In this sunshine state that surpasses the others
Because it does care and never smothers

The early morning brings the relief
That we need and gives us the feeling
That we can actually succeed
In a world where it's much too
Easy to see the grief

Sunshine out and I want to break out
You illuminate our lives
In all our days and in all our cries
Your radiance it does suffice

March 11, 2003

Unjustified War

The first casualty of an aggressive war
Is, as Dr. West says, truth
And that lack of truth will ultimately consume our youth
But the aggressors are always bent on how to torment
Torment the smaller countries of what they have and with a laugh
They do attack
With or without a pact
And if other countries hesitate
Because they foresee the violent impact of this injustice
They vote no,
This superpower will still go!
To fight to gain more
Of a resource that a particular country has in store
To add to its empire
You see, to gain and exploit from others that's what they require
So they go and knock down their door
And the guilt it leaves will later be felt
To the depth of humanity's core

March 18, 2003

My 28 Years

I reached 28 years of age and oh what I learned from this world
I've been witness to a lot of
Bitterness and poverty

Raised in the northwest part of town
Many from the other side
Would say it wasn't the best
But that's nothing to protest
Because the barrio, from whatever side, it is full of zest
But there needs to be more caress going
On in our families' nests

The young men in junior high
Many times aren't given the love
Not even a simple back rub
At times these overworked parents may try
But as the time goes by,
These kids get passed the sigh
And raise their pride up high

No longer do they need a hug
Because they cling to the thug
Who is more than willing to give them the drug
That will keep his family away but hey parents sadly enough
Someone must pay for those negative actions
That come about from the
Lack of love

March 9, 2003

The Bush and his Shrub

The Bush and his shrub can't stand Hussein in Iraq
That's why they want to lay down the smack
But what if by these actions the world it does crack?
And after they go in and this country they do smack
Will the U.S. later find itself in lack?
In lack of support and when it is weakened and can't purport
Will the U.N. release them from their spot with a note?
And then the U.S. might have to begin
Watching out for its ports?

March 18, 2003

The Tithe

Mr. Preacher if I couldn't pay my tithe
Will you not let me inside?
If you make salvation be based on this lie,
Then it would make the very angels weep and cry
But please don't give me some lies because in the end you'll have
to
Testify unto your maker
And if you don't tell the truth, he'll call on the baker
And well on your way you'll go all the way to the hole and
Be destined for the lashings
There you'll cry and yearn for compassion
But who'll be there to control your spasms?
So from the get go my brother look for your compassionate soul
And don't be those that contribute to burning the coal
That will see each of us die
And be consumed like a pie
And believe me that mindset won't be allowed in the sky
So please sigh
Before you answer this question and if the love of God is in your
soul
Then you won't feel tension and be willing to allow
My soul inside to be consoled
As you open the door
With a smile and hold your hand out in extension
Then we can walk through the door
And hold up our unity and ask the Lord for more
Faith and love
Because faith and love, in the end, are
What brings purity and will help
Us better reach the
Man up above

March 2, 2003

Learning To Be a Man

The journey to manhood is an eternal search
That for this brother was made easier by way of the church
When your father isn't there
You know, when you're a kid
The only thought that goes through your mind is no one cares
So you learn from the lessons that teach you
And sometimes the things that you do make you feel like a fool
Understand that these lessons are a stepping-stone,
You know a tool
And as the years go by, you grow
And the need for a father figure you don't need no mo'
And when you're feeling down and out
Or wanting to pout
Just know that in any situation there's always a way out
My progression towards manhood all took place in the hood
In all situations and tribulations, I was not done
Away with but stood

My search is continual even at 28
To me the ideal man to look up to would in him carry no hate
And in his goals would not hesitate
Or in the thought of questioning them contemplate
In his obligations he would not be late
He would be a man that's decisive
And of what he has is always willing to give.
God let me be a man that has these qualities
That way I may have that
Thing called peace

March 23, 2003

Career Day 2003 El Camino Jr. High

Always Fight to Achieve

Please open your ears and be ready to hear
Don't worry I'm not going to say anything to make you shed a
tear
Just listen to some of my thoughts
That I wrote down and brought
I hope you like them a little bit, no actually I hope you like them a
lot

El Camino students are capable of anything
All they have to do is put it in their mind that they can achieve
And in that mission don't stop until they succeed
Remember knowledge is always the key that will allow you to
better breathe

I understand that sometimes it might be difficult and "uncool" to
focus on your studies
But if you get ridiculed, I'd advice you to better pick your buddies
Because "Education is," as Mr. Muller says, "…the pathway to
success!"
But to get to that goal you must always try your best

Remember you must always try to keep reaching higher
So you can, at the end, stand as tall and strong as a Roman tower
So don't be someone that ends up being sour
Study and when you read every word please devour
Because that knowledge will ultimately give you the power

April 23, 2003

Pride comes before destruction

Proverbs 16:18 says, "Pride comes before destruction."
So for our own good
In pride we must do a sizeable reduction
How many are there with their pride up
High like a fifty foot wall?
Oh, when it comes down,
I don't want to see how hard you fall

If still you can't digest the message of this verse
Let's look at a man that saw the outcome of the fact
That he chose not by these words abide
St. Paul or Saul of Tarsus at first chose on a negative side to reside
Of the truth he turned his cheek
Not because he was meek
But because Jesus he was not yet ready or willing to seek
You see his stature, as a Pharisee, was one of power
So in his pride he did the Christians persecute
For anything even things of the most minute
Until one day on the now famous road to Damascus he was
forever changed
And he was released out of his
Prideful and unbelieving cage

So with the absence of pride
Humanity and reality no more do men
And women have
To hide

Be of good cheer

Mathew 14:27 says, "Be of good cheer
It is not good to be afraid."
Don't let those negative and crippling thoughts
Your mind raid
Or else if fear it is in your mind
It will make you a person
That to other people you can't trust
And so you'll resort to treat them unkind

Remember the book of Philippians
Which says, "rejoice now"
Go ahead that positive emotion
Yell as loud as a bell
And of these positive emotions
Please everyone go out and tell
Then of all the flowers you'll
Be able to enjoy their sweet smell

So, please my brother or sister be of good cheer
Remember to those bad thoughts
Don't lend an ear
But cast them to the back of your mind, you know to the rear

So if you start feeling afraid
Don't go to the nearest store to buy a beer
But cling to that wonderful message that is dear
And if that doesn't work
Just think of what the devil is
Wanting to do to your soul
And that is for it to
Burn and sere

Why must there be Suffering?

Why must there be suffering? I often ask myself
Maybe it's because I am filled with desire?
That's what the Buddhists say and if you deny this
Examine yourself closely
Who knows maybe you'll end up
Calling yourself a liar

Peace and harmony is the message from *Jah*
Why do mostly the poorest of the poor look for these qualities?
Maybe it's because they don't have hope for riches?
But is that valued more than peace?
I hope that's no the case because if it is, life has
Been such a waste and the only product
Produced has had a bad taste

Unity is what can lead people to a better sense of
Nationalism so that our lives can not be
Partitioned from that
Unnecessary schism

April 27, 2003

Will You Listen?

Aparteid what a system of division
That renders one people to make the unwise decision of putting
themselves on top and forcing others to clean until they say stop

The blacks and whites in S. Africa all can't take the pain of being
divided
And in that somehow feel pride in
One man named Mandela he tried to resist
But was soon thrown in jail by the ignorant racists

Men both black and white or brown and yellow should work to
show that they are all brothers. Does this pen reach anyone that is
the question? If it reaches one soul then this writing must not have
been dull, but I hope the words attack your conscious just like a
bull
Let's use these words to combat the actions and thoughts that
inspire such bad reactions

Mach 1, 2003

Love

I Wonder if You Will Ponder?
A collection of poems

Love in Corinthians

I Corinthians 13:8 says, "Love never fails."
So it'll get there
Even if it's late
At any rate
Don't be in anguish or build up your hate
Because before you know it there'll be your mate
Do you understand what I' saying or can't you relate?
If that's the case my brother or sister then build up your faith

Another verse in the book of Corinthians
Speaks of the love like for instance
So open you ears and be ready to listen
Cuz' when you hear it, there'll be no more need for division
Let me see what I'm thinking…or is there need for revision?
Oh that's right, I Corinthians 13:4 says if, "I have faith, so I
Could move mountains but have not love,
Then I am nothing."

Keep this small message wherever you go
Because that's what St. Paul wished us to know
And then when your courting you'll know where to row
Love is essential and not superficial
So put in your mind to reach cloud nine
Through these few love lines
Inspired from
The divine

March 2, 2003

What is the good life?

What is the good life?
What a perennial question
It lends itself to deep contemplation
But in the end that question always falls under subjection

Because who can tell you and I what is right?
How would we be able to prove they are bright?
And if I questioned would they put up a fight?
I know one thing that's for sure
And for me it is the cure
Love is the only variable that always endures
If you don't believe then stay for the tour
In the hearts of the believers of this emotion
It builds you up that it feels like an explosion

But love can only go so far
Because there are those whose minds and hearts are more focused
on things like golf
Or going to a bar
This is a sad sight but society informs me that there is little
sobriety
So I wonder where is the piety?
I must admit these are questions that I ask the almighty
But hey King Solomon said everything in this world was
meaningless
So does that make me think any less?
You must understand that I'm just trying to make sense of this
mess
That's why these thoughts that I have I can no longer suppress
The build up of the problems is much harder than playing chess
You see I'm trying to think what in this world would be best?

My heart tells me to keep on keeping on
Because the good life will not be prolonged
While you wait for it, just sing a song
Then you'll grow strong
So just go along
Because love when u find it is never wrong
What is the good life?
LOVE

February 22, 2003

Learn

I've lost you and that I know
They say that ultimately you "reap what you sew."
I guess then sadness and loneliness I rightfully deserve
But may the tears that now guide this pen
Be a testament to all of my fellow men

If that special person you have cuddled in your arms
Please don't do anything to bring to that
Beautiful heart any harm

May this message fall on opened ears
For all to hear
And may they follow a path that will bring about
A relationship that is sincere
So that the future with them
Will always be clear

June 10, 2003

Reflection of You

As I'm alone
And my hair I do comb
My thoughts begin to roam
About my time with you out in the town and at our home
And as my eyes look out the window
And listen to the birds sounds
I remember the day we went to the church to make our vows
How I wanted to shout that, "I loved you!" so loud
And then in my mind flashes another image of me moving out
Forever leaving our precious dream house
And then as the birds sing, another flash comes to
Me about when I felt compelled to take off the ring
That you put on me
That made me feel like a king
But now is no more than a dream
Because I threw it out in the sea
And has been consumed by the ocean and
When I did my heart
It did sting

March 19, 2003

Tonight the Sky

Tonight how lonely the sky looks on
It is quite a sad sight
As there is little light to illuminate the soul
It has evidently taken its toll
And the sight of the sky seems like
It's crying
And its sighing is enough to make
One feel like dying

Why does love carry one away?
It could happen any moment
As early as yesterday
Or today
Can one resist love?
Does one need it?
What a void it is without that other dove

What if there's a rainbow the day after?
Does that mean that in the future there'll be some laughter?
Truly it is best to live where there is plenty of sun
So it'll allow one's heart and soul to run
To the one that will
Love them a ton

March 9, 2003

Why does my heart hurt?

Why does my heart hurt?
Can it be from my own nature?
Or did it come from a female who had it in mind for it not to cure?
So in that malicious thinking maybe she did procure
To jinx me with a spell
That has made my heart feel not so well?
And thus that's why my heart pounds like a loud bell
That won't allow me the peace
That I seek
And I wonder will it only stop until I'm deceased?

Please Lord unto you I give you my problem
Because I know I definitely cannot solve it
I just ask one request
That you will give my the calm
That I felt when I was young, like when
I was being nursed by my mom
It is then that I'll be content
And, of the exterior problems of this world,
I won't care not one cent
Answer my prayer Lord
In all I have said, please know that
I have meant

April 25, 2003

Would You Care If I died?

Would you care if I died?
Or would I be in your life just another passerby?
Or would I be in your mind someone that did make you think?
Think in the most formal of situations
Or even as we shared 1, 2, or maybe 3 drinks
I want you to remember me as someone who had it in his heart to
do good
Wherever he stood
It would be the worst of deaths if I went out
Saying those lamentable words
"I should have…"
Because to me that would bring tears to my soul
And if that were the situation and I'm dying,
Who would my poor soul console?
I don't claim that I will accomplish everything I desire
But I want to always be reaching higher
And for me I resort to a higher power
So that for those that knew me, knew that I was
A man of compassion and love
If that is the case, I will go
In peace to be with the
Man up above

March 19, 2003

Tonight you bring about the saddest lines...

Tonight you bring about the saddest lines...
I remember being together in the Jacuzzi
Feeling the warmth of your presence
I must tell you that I was captivated by the bubbles of your essence
When I think of the laughter that we shared, I have to say it was
surreal
so much so that it would fill the most eloquent singing birds like a
meal
But that moment is no more which
Causes my voice to loose its pitch
And I wonder would the chances of having you still with me
Be greater if I were rich?

Tonight you bring about the saddest lines...
Even though Pablo Neruda felt he had sadder lines than I,
I can promise you that that is a lie
I say this not to harass
But to show that this heart was in a relationship that would prove
not to last
And even though her heart was superficial
My life in that time was beneficial
And for that alone these lines that I now write are very special
But just thinking of you
The pain that my heart feels makes me want to yell
And for that I would form a pact with the
Devil just to take off this evil spell

Tonight you bring about the saddest lines...
Although you held up your fight
Great knight
Understand that she's out of your sight
It has just hit me that these indeed
Are the saddest lines tonight
Because my heart with you sees no light

48

And because my pen sees and understands the
Pain that you are putting me through
Refuses to continue to write

March 3, 2003

You Are Appreciated

Having spent time with you
Has truly been a dream come true
You were someone that had caught my attention
And to my Colombian friend, some years back, this I had
mentioned
I had no idea that after some time together in a bubbly pool
You would give me the opportunity of your body to soothe
You came to me with an awesome agreement that to me was
amazing
And you my body has since been craving

I remember when we first made our way to my room
I couldn't help but think of the ecstasy that would follow soon
And so my soul felt cool
As my love you did consume

When I feel your body under mine
Man, how it blows my mind
So, in turn, your lips I do kiss in a way that is kind
All the while my heart is saying "My, My, My!"

With this being said, it is fair to say that you for anyone would be
a catch
But don't allow just anyone your heart to snatch
Even you could swear that they are your match
You girl are a beautiful jewel
So please don't let anyone treat you in a way that is cruel
Because I'll tell you something they are nothing but fools

I appreciate the love you have given me
A better man you have definitely made me
I thank you for your company
It has been for me the perfect remedy
(S.N.)

March 27, 2003

Love Poem

The smile that you carry on your face must have been heaven sent
That as of late has had me bent out of shape
I know that you're thinking that I am a liar
But can't you see that I'm trying to admire?
That smile of yours oh how it inspires!
And those pretty lips and eyes
They do have me mesmerized!
They are definitely, for me, the ideal prize

If you do not think that I am sincere
Just look in my eyes and you'll see that they're clear
They're clear and they're looking at someone who they think is
dear
And these lips of mine would like nothing more than to
Whisper sweet love verses in your ear

I am glad we were able to meet
You have many qualities that make you so sweet
And thus easy to greet
I have to admit that your beauty makes me nervous
But I want you to know that I'm here at your service

This last verse I'll tell you but please will you listen?
Can't you see you're what I've been missin'
This next line I'll say today and everyday
That my wish of you will come true as I pray
The words I would say is Lord please let her stay
That is of course if it's in our fate
This poet has one last line to say
Before it gets late
So please won't you wait?

If ever there was a puddle in our way
I want you to know that
I would lay down my cape for
You any day

February 27, 2003

Look Into My Eyes

Look into my eyes and you will see that they're serious
The love that they feel for you will you think of as curious?
For these thoughts that I now reveal please don't be furious

If you look into these eyes
You will see to the depths and see that when they look back at you
they want to sigh
Because the love that they feel for you it is true
I know I'm a fool for feeling blue
But you the gates of my heart have opened up and you it wants to
pursue

You're looking at the depths of my soul
And seeing the suffering that you're causing, will you not console?
This heart of mine you did take and stole
That love that I had in store
Just know that your eyes to me I see like a prize
They do much to entice
But the thoughts that I have about having you in my room will
that be seen as a vice?
I know that later I will pay the price
I'll be on my knees enduring all the pain, as I'm praying to Christ

March 11, 2003

In the Morning

Awakening in the morning and having you by my side
Made my eyes want to cry
And this love that I felt inside,
I prayed to God it would never die

When your eyes they look at me
I can see that to me they do admire
And that is all I need for this heart to feel inspired

And when your lips they do touch my chest
That's when I want to fulfill my quest
Which will give both our souls some rest
Do you feel what I'm saying?
Or your emotions are you trying to suppress?

When the morning comes around, it's time for me to leave
Just know that my soul, after this passionate night, it does feel
relieved
So I leave
but don't ever forget about the love that this night allowed to be
conceived

June 13, 2003

The Clown

How many times have I been let down
By girls that made me feel like a clown?
Sometimes when I'm dealing with a diss,
I must allow what you did to be dismissed
Or at least end it with a soft kiss…

But maybe I'm wrong
And have been thinking too long?
If that's the case,
Then give me a taste
Of those pretty lips as I hold on to that waist
So that I may leave and save face
And not feel disgraced
Of this love that
Was misplaced

March 1, 2003

Why do you come and make yourself known?

Why do you come and make yourself known?
When the time it has taken me to forget you has taken much
moans
Even though I loved you in the past,
Your love, to the ocean, I have cast

That is not to say that I don't want you as a friend
I just need to not let you into the gates of my heart,
So that my soul can mend
And not in a negative direction
Later be sent

June 13, 2003

Reality Flee From Me

My heart can't stand the reality
That, to your heart, I have lost the key
That has allowed me to dream such sweet dreams
And in love wholeheartedly believe

Oh reality flee from me
That present picture I don't want to see
I'd rather live in the past
Knowin' your heart still wants and dreams
With the belief that our love will always be
And you in my arms I can
Once again feel relief

June 10, 2003

End to My Grieving

The day you walked into my life
That's when an end was put to all of my strife
And for the second time in my life
I contemplated the notion of once again having a wife

Although I felt weary about this feeling
I didn't reject it because I knew I would end up grieving
And so in your presence my soul was relieving
And in the chance to have my soul mate
My heart actually began believing

Please forgive me if because I'm cautious, it seems like I don't love
you
I do love you but I need to be certain
That what you tell me is not a facát and that your true intentions
are not actually hidden behind a dark curtain
Because if I fell into that trap again I know that
My heart would not take it for certain
And it would die from
All the hurtin'

May 3, 2003

Is this justice?

Is this justice?
I'm here looking out into my new backyard
Dried grass and seats turned upside down
Sometimes looking at my situation
My face it does turn into a frown
And in my mind there's nothing
But deep contemplation
But still I must ask why?
I followed the "rules" that go with a
Sacred union so how or why did
I not fulfill your needs?
Was I dealing with a lost cause to
Begin with, a weed?
I shake my head in despair
I could have sworn to God that
Our love was not any ordinary thing
I really thought it was rare
But, in the end, you to my heart were not
Considerate and it you didn't seem to
Take care of one bit
So, with no answer to this question
I must accept and move on
Just singing a song
And not worrying about
How I felt that
I was wronged

To My Dear Friend

Black hair, beautiful smile, and sparkling eyes
That's how I remember you by
Oh, those moments of friendship that we spent in Vegas were
supreme
A time that was so fun it leaves me wondering was it a dream?

The time was well spent there at the Hilton Las Vegas, having a
blast
Before we went out on the town
We knew no matter what happened we would not feel down
And not once did we frown

I had the most incredible temptation to hold your hips
And progress to kiss those pretty lips
But I didn't because well I knew if I did I would feel passion down
to my fingertips

I loved your outgoing attitude because it uplifts and compliments
mine
Which is why I felt a need to try
But I felt if I tried it would not be accepted but rejected
So I was resolved to let another crush go dejected
Until a Monday morning, I felt I was touched by the Lord
And there you were pretty as ever
Making me feel like I had finally reached heaven
And from then on I've experienced
Some real living
(S.N.)

February 22, 2003

Don't Suppress Your Emotions

These thoughts of yours why do you suppress?
Do you think that by doing so the heart
Of this man it will impress?
I will tell you the truth
I will care somewhat less
Because it will leave me thinking,
"Will she be indifferent to my caress?"

So girl, try your best
And that unhealthy advice and your past put to rest
That way you'll be happy in that your nest
Believe me in everything you do
You will feel less stress

March 19, 2003

This heart of Mine

Few people come into this heart of mine
That when it happens I feel it's a sign
It's a sign because there are clues left behind
The clues that I find are sometimes enlightening
But the touch of your body that is like lightning
You're precious, sweet, and soft
Man I wish we were up in a loft
In our make believe mansion
We would experience some serious passion
Our hearts yeah they would be smashin'
The gates of this heart are left open for you
Because I want you to know that you can pursue
Any life that you choose without any concerns
So please discern
My love in turn
But I want you to know that if I'm not in your heart
It won't bother me to
Pack up and part

March 1, 2003

To My Asian Pilot

Pilots are made in the air above land
But love manifested itself in the heart of this man
Yeah, I knew it was impossible the day I first saw you
But I had always told myself that you would come true

Those Asian eyes are like two crystal balls that can hypnotize
Because when I look into them, I can see into the future
And see many beautiful sights
That makes me feel so strong an emotion
Out of your love potion

The laughter and your voice
Teases me like girls normally do to boys
But it's something that I enjoy
The sweet melody of your words do much to encourage
That being said they give me much courage

Although you could sometimes be rude
I look past that because at the root
That's not who you are
Only when you're sub par
Very few times in this world does one find
Someone to complete them for real
So much so that if one does experience it
They'd even be willing to steal

Love will ultimately stand the test of time
If it doesn't then just laugh because it wasn't to be
It wasn't to be but don't worry, jubilee
The time spent together was better than having not that memory
To be able to write to you out of the blue
You see that's the key
(S.N.)

February 22, 2003

The Promise

If I promise to be loyal
Will your heart my actions spoil?
I will try with all of my heart to
Act in a way that is royal
So that in the end there won't be anger
That will cause your blood to boil
So, in my goal to be loyal, I will always
Persistently and
Diligently toil

June 10, 2003

The Cure

The day I first saw you my heart was yours
And right then I knew that for all my troubles you were my cure
Trust what I say
All that I ask is that you stay by my side
And when I go somewhere you come for the ride

You are the flower
That occupies my every hour
And gives me the power
To stand as tall and strong as a Roman tower
Just to think of my life without you, it would definitely be sour
If you feel the same way, then don't be ashamed
But come to me so that
I don't go insane

Feb 28, 2003

Thank You

You have stuck it out
And helped me out
Through all the problems that many times made
Me furious and wanting to pout
You know something, you've been there
When many have never cared
And you were a good listener when I laid out my heart until it was
bare
So the fact that you showed concern tells me that people like you
are rare
If I were to stack up all of my tribulations and the madness that
you helped me face and not run
The weight would be so great that it would weigh a ton
People like you are to me a great treasure
Because the love and compassion that you show can never be
measured
So I leave you with this last line
The fact that I was able to meet you has changed me forever
So I know that it's been
More than a sign

March 30, 2003

The Love that is Professed

In any love relationship,
Always look at the actions that follow
The love that is professed
Because they do much to confess
They confess to you of a love that is real
Or to show that being with you they really don't feel

If that's the case, don't protest
But find a girl that will pass this test
And will free your heart from all that confusion
And give you some
Much-needed rest

June 13, 2003

The worst pain to feel

What is the worst pain to feel?
The type that everyone wants to conceal?
It's not the type that makes you feel embarrassed
But the one that makes you feel the absence
Of that much needed love caress
Do you feel what I'm expressing?
If not, wait and you'll hear more about this pain
That now my soul and heart it is pressing
When I close my eyes and I go to my dream town
I awake to those two lovely eyes that do much to my soul suffice
As her head it does rest on my chest
And her thoughts and love to me they fully express
That's when my soul is full of zest
So we awaken and after breakfast
We go to the woods to, from this world take a rest in
And as I hold you, I don't care if this world all around us it does
go away
All I know is I want you with me to stay
So we can go to our room and in our arms both lay
We can be together in our bed for as long as a week
It that's the case, everything in this world I won't care about
Or seek because it's all just a rat race
So I plead with my dream to just let me hold her a minute more
Before I do awake and am left to travel in this world alone
Through this world that at times dishes out much hate
That leaves me hoping of coming back to my dream
That can give me the one and only relief
That is what I need to feel that in the future, it might
Actually come to fruition and be conceived
And that, that girl I can actually one day hold in my arms
I would do whatever for her even move to some remote dwelling
She would definitely be a great prize to hold
That would be made even more perfect when my
1st born comes into this world

And I'm allowed to see my own eyes
It is then that I know my pain
Would subside

You are so cold

Even as you asked me to be with you
I always obliged
Because I hold dear your emotions
And if I didn't want to I made an honest
Effort to let you off easy
I never wanted you to think of me as sleazy
But as a gentleman
Someone that was different from the others
But it seems that to treat me coldly to you it doesn't bother

Yeah, it hurt my heart to hear your response to my advance
You see rejections is something that is hard for me to stand
But I am a man
So this cold rejection I must take
Whether it means that I have to drink a six-pack of beer by the
lake
I just miss hearing your lovely voice
It definitely made me feel a deep poise
As I had you by my side
Oh how I enjoyed having you by me as you rode in my ride
But now my heart must deal with that hard and cold message
From your heart that towards me
Aims no more
And that's okay because it
Will allow me to look more easily
For the warmness that will
Give me the much-needed
Caress

Actions Explored

If I could move back the hands of time,
I would go back to when you were mine
I know when I hurt your heart it did feel it to the core
And even though I tried to keep my heart cold
My conscious it did torment me after my actions I explored
Not that what I did was socially unacceptable
It's just that I tend to look at life through conscientious spectacles
And my soul is always searching to live for a higher moral
That way I can alleviate giving myself
Or other people unnecessary sorrow

June 10, 2003

What do I despise in a person?

What do I despise in a person?
So much so that my soul to them it is cursin'?
I despise someone who purports to be my friend
But through their mouth it's another message they send
When they see you, yeah they tell you hi and goodbye
Why do they put up that face and lie?
From all that hypocrisy,
My soul just
Sighs

May 14, 2003

When did love first bloom?

When did love first bloom?
Was it that afternoon in June
When we observed the moon?
Sometimes I wish that you'd come home soon
If you come to my room
I'll have to consume
That deep appetite
That'll make us feel just right
But don't worry I'm not out to fight
I just want to love you with all of my might
So please be polite
As I show and profess my love to you,
With this pen as I now write

When your flower to me it did bloom,
That's when I came out of my doom
But now as I stand next to this flower
I realize the smell
And its smell is quite sour
As I look closer, I realize that it was all a trick
Because it was always a weed that was trying to deceive
But now has come to its end
As I look up, I realize that just straight ahead there is my flower
That was destined, in my life, to tower
Tower above all the roses
No matter what they try and reveal through all of their poses
What I know for sure is that she was for me
On that at least I hope, after listening to
My heart, do you agree?

April 27, 2003

In the Courtyard

Out in the courtyard that is where we met
When you looked at me I knew I would fall into your net
So I tried to resist your essence
Anyway that I could but it was impossible
You have a magnetic presence

The way in which your eyes looked at mine
It was sublime
I must admit I lost track of time
Then a flood of poetic lines came to my mind
Because I saw you as kind
And I thought would you mind?
So I dropped you a line
I don't know my mind was going so
Fast it might have been nine?

Whatever the case,
When I looked at your lips I wanted to taste
If ever we meet again in the yard,
I will try especially hard
Maybe I'll give you a card?
Just be real with me
If you're interested cool,
If not then please let me be
If you don't want me I'd rather
Spend time with the bees
Than to know that I'm
Being deceived

March 9, 2003

Why I love the night

Why do I love the night?
It is there that I see the most beautiful sight
When I close my eyes that is when my heart it awakens
By your soft touch
How I want to embrace you and love you so much
It has been an eternity since my hands traced the outline of your
face
And your lips how they feel so sweet
I'm so very glad that they were
Able to meet

Darkness brings light to my soul
And that light it does burn through the night like a hot coal
When you make your way to my bed
There really is nothing more to be said
Life has no value all around us
Because
We both through the night have reached Nirvana
And before the night is over I hold your wrists and look into your
eyes
Because sadly I know that that time with you must suffice
And slowly, from me, you begin to fade
And my hand it tries to bring you into my arms
But reality begins to knock on my door
And then as I go and open the doors
That's when my soul begins thinking that it doesn't
Have you and so let's out a deep roar
Because love will have to wait until
The next night so that my heart can
Once again soar
And once again see
That beautiful sight that will
Open those precious
Love doors

July 6, 2003

You give me might

I love to hold your waist very tight
You know you give me a lot of might
So much so that I feel I can take anyone on in any fight
And if ever I get caught up in any plight
I know that you will always be there to comfort
Me and in what I should do
You will counsel me in what is right

I feel that you care for me deeply
But if you don't want me to think badly of you
Please don't ever deceit me
If that is the case,
You, my heart will erase
Erase from that part of my heart that is at the base
I don't think you will ever do that
Because you know that
I will not be
Anyone's mat

April 25, 2003

How long will your love last?

You look at me with such sincere eyes
That leaves me wondering is it a disguise?
Or maybe you are somehow blinded by your past?
But my dear pen why be so pessimistic?
It's time that you start being optimistic
And putting more of your trust in your mate
Who knows maybe she's got the ingredient that will bring about
those happy moments you know that ones that are easy to relate
But if you are only here for a bit
I hope when you leave, I stay in your heart in a way that you
won't think of as sick
My heart says please don't go away from me
Because you have entered into a zone that I don't allow many to
see
My heart is at your feet
and is always willing when
It sees you to greet

April 25, 2003

I don't want to understand you

I don't want to understand you
Because what you do is cruel
What you do and tell me
Are two different things
Man, this is so confusing that I don't know what
To do to better understand you
At times, I've resorted to taking classes at school
To know what are the rules
But even all that psychology
Does nothing to help alleviate myself of your pathology
And I wonder why after such disillusionments
Do I accept your apologies?

March 26, 2003

My L.O.V.E.

Many girls have passed through this heart
You, however, my heart has not allowed to part

Leave and the pain I will feel I cannot conceive
Only you have been able to this soul relieve
Vow, would you, to not take another course or deceive
Every thought of mine is centered around your beauty because
you are my cutie

March 16, 2003

El A.M.O.R.

Eres la mujer ideal para mi
La muchacha que Dios me mando porque se que yo no te escoji

Antes de realizar cuanto te queria, no tenia mucho interes el día
Mujer sublime dime que quieres quererme
O dejame saber que no va ser, para buscar el poder
Rudy se llama este corazón, que bien sabe que en el amor no se
mete la razón

16 de marzo del 2003

Mujer

Mujer tu savez que to quiero
Que sin ti talvez me muero
Pero quiero que sepas que este amor que
siento en verdad que es sincero
Y que te quiero para mi
Anda, dime que si

Cuantas veces yo e pensado que hace tiempo
atras yo a ti te deberia deber robado
Pero no cumplí con mi recado
Quiero que sepas que siempre
estaré a tu lado

1 de abril del 2003

Lips come together for Only a While

Lips come together
In whatever weather
Love chooses two people to unite
Into a harmonious union that
Makes them feel just right

Even though we were only together for a while
At our height, I would walk however many miles
Just to be with you even if it's only for a while
The expression on my face when we are
Together would always be a smile
Because you have
A great style

February 22, 2003

If I call you will you answer?

If I call you will you answer?
Or will you just look at the number and not bother
Come on girl I'm not trying to smother I just want to hook up,
You know be your lover
And make some passionate love under the covers
Can't you see? I want to give you company
Or just lend an ear to the problems you have with your mother
So if I call and you hear a ring
Come on now answer my queen
Cuz' it's your king who wants nothing more
Than to make you
Feel supreme

March 23, 2003

Why did you fall for me when you did?

Why did you fall for me when you first did?
If you might have ignored me, yeah I might have cried like a kid
But that's better than suffering the torment of not having you in
my crib

They say that after a fling gone bad it's better to turn and laugh
like a clown
Than to sit by the way and let yourself drown
So don't frown
Rejoice now

I cherish the times that we had together
Under the weather
Believe it or not the time with you felt better
Than just having spent those times reading other peoples love
letters

The times out on the town were something amazing
I was caught up in your aura just craving
I was craving to get you alone in my room
You see that was a fantasy I wanted to realize soon
Before I met my doom,
In my tomb
So you see you were always in my plan
Man, we had so much fun!
But just know that no matter what
I will always cherish
You a ton

March 2, 2003

Tell me

I want to look at you and feel that you love me
So tell me right now to give me relief
Why do I have to question your love?
Maybe it's a sign from the man up above
Maybe I need a different type of dove?

When we were first drinking a beer
Right there right by the pier
I told myself that you seemed sincere
You might say that maybe I'm
Saying this because I drank liquor
But the next day without you I must
Admit my heart felt much sicker
So tell me about your future plan
Does it include this man?

March 1, 2003

Spring Love

Spring love is the best time of the year
It's a time when flowers begin to bloom
And the birds singing, Oh! It's beautiful these sounds that one
consumes

Something about the freshness in the air
Makes many people want to care
The love that they feel is really unreal
And this love is so contagious that it's impossible to conceal

That being said the girl is the one that is led to the point of
accepting him as her guy
And it's then that he let's out a sigh
But he doesn't give in, in totality
Because sadly he knows of the reality
Of the volatility of women so he embraces the moment's pleasure
And for that moment he knows he is sure
And thus decides he's willing to accept the consequence
Of opening his heart and the outcome endure
Knowing full well that the
Spring is at fault for
How it allures

Mach 9, 2003

Your Love

How can you profess your love so much to me?
Don't you understand what you put me through?
If not then come listen to my thoughts and see
At first, you were my dream come true
The love that my mind had many times in the past tried to pursue

Then, it happened that you asked me to your mind and soul
relieve
And although, at first, your supplication I could not believe
With time, that old crush that I had for you my heart it once again
began to conceive
And in your arms I felt much relieved

You came at a time when I needed a sincere companion to hold
and you weren't afraid to in me confide
And to your rules and values I wanted to abide
But later I saw that that lifestyle I could not live because my true
thoughts and beliefs could not be fully expressed
Because we were at a stage in our lives
Where we were trying to make sense of our individual situations
You know, how to deal with our pasts and survive
And when you expressed to me that you thought I would cheat
I promised not to deceit
And I didn't when we were a couple,
But other people came between our friendship and created much
rubble
If in the future we meet,
With all of my heart, you I will with fond
Memories greet

June 13, 2003

Lover's Prayer Addendum

Otis Redding had a lover's prayer
In it he sang from his heart
It was not that he was smart
But he followed that spot in his heart
that was hit by a lover's dart

I also have my own lover's prayer that I want to share
After you left and made your break
I wanted to drive through my heart this metal stake
Because I don't want to start over again
Beginning another clean slate
So Lord, please listen to my plea
As I release from my pen all these lonely tears
That are creating their own sea
Please, save me from this love disease
That I have been dealing with and I want to
Put an end to and finally cease
Please Lord give me a release
I want my heart to live in peace
So if you hear my prayer please bring me that girl
That will calm my needs
And will allow me to in love again
Wholeheartedly believe

July 2, 2003

Happy B-Day

I wish you a happy birthday on this your day
I'm sure that the angels will always
Be by your side to stay
And if that you ever question,
Just let me mention
That my hand for you, you will
Always find in
Extension
(S.N.)

May 14, 2003

Will you fight to find love?

Will you fight to find love?
You know that girl that you always want to
Massage and give a back rub
Is this a necessary emotion?
Or has it all been blown out of proportion?
Whatever the case
Always look for love at the base
Whether it means finding someone of a different race
Just know what you want so that your
Precious time you
Won't waste

March 23, 2003

Could it be?

When I looked out into the distance and saw your
Beautiful eyes look back at me
I asked myself could it be?
She must have definitely been sent to me from the man up above
Who all things can see
Then, when I released a poem from my heart,
Her ears I knew were open and my words to her they aimed
They aimed and hit at the center of her heart
And it was then that I knew that her attention
From me would not part
And apparently they did her soul console

And when she came up to me and told
Me she liked my poem
Man, I felt positive sensations and
My heart's thoughts began to in a
Positive direction roam

June 1, 2003

The Arrangement

When we were together for a week,
The time flew by just like drum beat
Even though I know it was for a short time,
I must admit you captivated my mind
I never imagined I'd write these lines
Many might say that it's even a crime
I write these lines to you to get your attention
Because I want you to know I appreciate your affection

Sometimes I wish we could still make passionate love
Until or bodies erupted
Such a shame that apparently after a meaningless night your
attraction towards me just faded
So I was left feeling jaded
What confuses me though about all this is that very little was
stated

But hey I guess that's how it goes but I want you to know that my
doors will still be open for you
That is if you choose
If you don't then don't worry I'm not the type of man to pout
At least not out loud
I'm just a curious poet that doesn't mind writing a few love lines
to the one that has captivated his mind
With an arrangement,
Which he looked at in amazement
This arrangement was one he thought might last
But now seems like a distant look in the past

Sometimes I feel like an outcast
But I know that deep down
I will triumph at last

February 27, 2003

Did She Care for Me?

I wonder if she really cared for me?
What a tough question it must be
Because if you must ask it
Then you must have experienced a lack of it
But never feel down about your situation
Because there's a lot of temptation,
Which can give you great sensations
That have been around since the beginning of creation

Just remember that everything that is done to you
Will surely come around to the subject that brings you down
So don't frown
Or put down
Just go about town
In a way that
Is sound

Your Lips

When I kiss your lips
My problems are erased from my mind
And in our interactions
Much grows my attraction
And thus my lust it wants some action
Without later any
Negative reactions

May 3, 2003

My doorstep

When I saw you at my doorstep
I wondered could it be that such
a beauty could come to me?
I must admit I stood
There in disbelief

As time went by
And our thoughts coincided
I could feel that your intentions resided
They resided in a state of bliss
And someone who I knew I would later miss
So I made the most out of every kiss
Until with time this passerby love of yours slowly subsided
But those memories and times together are kept in my mind
And our courtship and friendship
Is something I will
Never hide

Do I Love You?

Do I love you or not?
That's the question that I ask myself a lot
Then, just when I think I know the answer
Me and you become involved in another disaster,
Which sends my heart into a whirlwind trying to understand
How in the world this mess occurred?
Some of these fights are truly absurd
But still this question I must ask
And to answer it is truly
The ultimate task

May 14, 2003

Volatile Women

Yeah you say you want me in bed
And that you did get
But have you done your homework or even read?
The act that you seek
Brings out emotions
So how can you expect for this man not to feel a commotion?
After having made you his
And given his love to you
Yeah, the feeling for me was true

So we shared some intimate moments
Come on now don't lament
Because if you do that'll cause me a deep torment
Because my body cannot have you here
Do you hear what I am saying? Do these words sere?
If so then just know that this is what I'm thinking
And because I've said this it's not to hurt you and lead you to go
drinking
But to know that this
Arrangement it is
Stinking

March 11, 2003

Are you the one for me?

Are you the one for me?
That is what I ask
Because I want to avoid falling on my ass
Which has happened in the past
By girls who had less than class

The type of personality for me
Let me see
She has to be spontaneous, outgoing and gracious
Because that's what makes me tenacious

I refuse to say I'm nice and polite
Because that cliché has lost all of its might
Give me a girl that is spunky and free of lies
I will take her to Vegas so we can jump in a pool
And have a few drinks right there by the side
Then we'll go to the casinos and on the black jack table she can
kiss my dice
And later in the bedroom I will make love to her even as it rains
And I won't finish until I feel that she has came
Then as we go back to the strip, her neck I will lick
As I hold on to her waist my love it does want another taste
So after the night wears out
We ignite our love
And who cares if the neighbors they do hear our sounds?
A girl with this type of personality is what I need
Do you hear me or does that not fit your creed?
Then let me know so I can look elsewhere because in
This mission of mine I must succeed

Do you see what I mean?
If not girl then you'd better eat your beans
And then not only will you be lean
But will have the wisdom to answer in a way that is keen

But hey don't make a scene
If you are that girl, however, then let yourself be seen
Who knows maybe you are my queen?

February 23, 2003

There You Go

There you go doing the same thing you said you wouldn't do
Come on girl do you do it alone
Or are you motivated by your crew?
There you go saying you're independent
A woman with no attachments
I find it hard to understand your way of thinking
Your rationing doesn't make sense
As a matter of fact it sounds like pure nonsense
Having your separate ambitions from mine that's fine
But saying that they're all separate from mine?
Come on now, you're walking a fine line
believe me I'm trying to talk to you and think of you in a way
that's kind
But what comes out of your mind just blows my mind
forcing me to resort to these straight forward rhymes
Because if I don't who knows I might go out and commit some
dumb crime
And I know all too well that that'll cost me my hide
But I will stop here for a lack to time
But through these writings, I express these thoughts of you that
I must admit run chills down my spine
But I'm consoled knowing that the other
Part of my soul I
Will soon find

March 18, 2003

Excuse Me Miss

Excuse me Miss
I've got a list
So I need your ears to be crisp
Yeah, I'll try to speak without a lisp
And don't deny cuz' I'll insist
And believe you me I will persist
I've been watching you cuz' you are fine
And in my mind
This fantasy won't let me be
So por favor dime que si?

You and me
In my room
Our passions will be consumed
And after we'll go
And take a stroll
But my appetite is big and I still want more
Cuz' I adore you to the core
Your essence I will explore
From head to toe
And I won't stop until we explode
And you'll know when it happens because you'll hear my roar
Then we can go and hit the road
And whenever you need me, well you
Know my number code

March 16, 2003

Crazy Woman

I invite you to listen to my truest thoughts and truest feelings
about those women classified as crazy, who have this man bent
out of shape.
The Crazy woman does nothing but destroy the virtuous man of
everything he sees as right. Never ever should a man say he
knows how to choose a dove
Because the mind, which reasons goes only to the doorstep of love

And from there seizes but from there the heart takes
Over and all reasoning is out the window
What a shame for the man whose heart goes blinded and is left to
suffer the anguish of a crazy woman that is of less value than an
ant in a man's bedroom.
A crazy woman will not know what she wants in life but that's not
the bad part. The bad part is that she will let her confusion out on
you and focus her confusion on you. That I'm convinced is not
love but a scapegoat. If she doesn't hesitate to not talk to you or
return your calls and is quick to argue with you then know heart of
mine that that never was love in the first place but lust and that
should never be confused with love, better to focus on the body
and never the eyes. That is the truth in its essence
And please this heart of mine listen and erase her from your
memory for your own sake, come on now reason make your
presence
Crazy woman why don't you leave my mind it seems like I'm
walking a fine line, walking through this world only wishing to see
your eyes
And oh how slow the time flies
In those precious hours. Why does someone sweet attract to
someone sour?
I'm searching and searching for some higher power
To put me at ease and let me feel that great emotion we all know
as peace

Crazy woman release your grips from me,
Please let me be free
From your bondage so I can sit back and relax as I drink a cup of
tea.
Don't you know that you have me held hostage. You're probably
happy because the spell that you have cast has proven itself to last.
Crazy woman with no emotions do you feel bad or maybe even
sad
At what you've done Or do you wish to finish me off I know it'll
make you glad? If you do love me…Wait a minute! What am I
saying?
Can't I see that because of you I've been payin'
Through my emotions, which has me now on my knees praying
Crazy woman you knew how to play the game, which I never
knew until it came
Then I felt lame
But it's all the same
Because I know when I reach fame
Your name I shall never defame
Because at least out of the caressing came one fine lesson
That in this heart will remain

March 7, 2003

Arrangements

What a crazy thing arrangements are
You come together
Under the weather
For a specific thing
Knowing well that it does not involve a ring
With that being said,
the two jump in bed
They explore their bodies throughout wanting to bring fulfillment
to each other
You see that's what the encounter's about

It's true that love is a real thin line
Just when you think it couldn't happen to you
Your friend will be witness that you're walking around looking
blue
But it shouldn't be a surprise I'm sure
If you look closely you would have seen some of the clues
And if you need console in your heart, then turn to the blues
As many have done to have their feelings soothed

An arrangement ultimately brings a little relief
After a divorce and a few friendships
It'll allow you to look out into the world through more
experienced lenses

Departures are a must we all know too well
And the sex, well it was great
Spending time with this mate
She made me relate
Each night as we
Stayed up late

Feb 28, 2003

102

Union

The magnets of love bring two bodies in lust
Sucking and kissing erases all the stressing
That this world brings you know those problems and things

Yeah, this emotion of love satisfies the appetite
Which makes two people become one in a union that feels so right
And in their embrace they hold on so tight
In this dark thing we call night

Those moments of bliss and ecstasy
Are for all our problems the perfect remedy
And it gives us a break from
All the calamity

March 11, 2003

Analysis

No matter what the world says about what I think about you,
I will continue to direct my heart in a way that shows that my
thoughts are pure
I could never and would never want to live a life if I didn't feel it
was true
I want to live it to the full
And believe me to get there, I would use every tool
You are the one that has entered into the deepest corner in my
heart that has left me feeling vulnerable to an extent
Because I ask myself "What if you really aren't sincere and in your
feelings towards me you later lament?
Then my thoughts start to racing like would you really care one
cent if the only thing I could promise you was a tent?
Or are you really the nice person that you seem?

But I will stop analyzing
Because it could in itself be paralyzing
Paralyzing to the mind
What I need to do more is synthesizing our love so we can
progress and not regress
I want to alleviate our present situation
Because I think about you on every occasion
But I don't want this to be for you a persuasion
I just want you to look back at our past
In a pleasant reflection

April 27, 2003